The only thing new in the world
is the history you don't know.

— Harry Truman

Making Better Concrete

Guidelines to Using
Fly Ash for Higher Quality,
Eco-Friendly Structures

By Bruce King, P.E.

GREEN BUILDING PRESS
The Art & Science of Building Well

ON THE COVER:
The Pantheon in Rome, built by the Emperor Hadrian c. 180 AD
using Roman concrete: pozzolanic soils and lime –
virtually the same thing as high fly ash concrete

Copyright 2005 by Bruce King

All rights reserved. No part of this book may be reproduced in any form or by any electronic or
mechanical means, including information storage and retrieval systems, without permission
in writing from the publisher, except by a reviewer who may quote passages in review.

First Edition

Published by Green Building Press, PO Box 6397, San Rafael, California 94903
www.greenbuildingpress.com
SAN pending, see www.greenbuildingpress.com

Manufactured in the USA
Printed on recycled paper

Illustrations by the author
Edited by Carol Venolia
Design by Debra Turner
Proofreading and stunning insights by Sarah Weller King

Library of Congress Cataloging-in-Publication Data
Bruce King
Making Better Concrete: Guidelines to Using Fly Ash for Higher-Quality, Eco-Friendly Structures
Summary: Guidelines to Using Fly Ash for Higher-Quality, Eco-Friendly Structures
ISBN 0-976-4911-0-9
1. Concrete 2. Fly Ash 3. Green Building 4. High Volume Fly Ash Concrete

TABLE of CONTENTS

A. Pozzolans defined by source and standards organizations
Class N, Class C, Class F
Proposed simplified standard:
Loss On Ignition (LOI), Particle Size, and Strength Activity Index (SAI)

B. Pozzolans defined by reactivity and availability
1. Cementitious and highly active pozzolans
   Ground granulated blast furnace slag, aka "slag"
   Class C fly ash

2. Highly active pozzolans
   Silica fume
   Rice Hull Ash (RHA)
   Metakaolin

3. Normal pozzolans
   Class F (low-calcium) fly ash
   Natural pozzolans

4. Weak pozzolans
   Industrial by-products
   Natural materials

The basic pozzolanic reaction

The transition zone

A. Effects of fly ash on fresh concrete
1. Reduced water demand
2. Reduced bleed water
3. Increased workability and pumpability
4. Continuing slump

B. Effects of fly ash on plastic concrete
1. Extended set times
2. Reduced heat of hydration
3. Reduced plastic shrinkage cracking

C. Effects of fly ash on hardened concrete
    1. Slower rate of strength gain
    2. Reduced permeability
    3. Reduced drying shrinkage
    4. Resistance to scaling from deicing salts

Appendices

Dedicated

to

P. K. Mehta

and

V. M. Malhotra

for seeing the big picture
and doing something about it

It took me until I was this old
to figure out what not to play

– Dizzy Gillespie

PREFACE

Many people have dedicated their careers to understanding and recording the enormously complex subject of concrete in general, and of fly ash concrete in particular. We owe them great thanks for their contribution to the public good. There are also many architects, engineers, and builders who are willing to try new materials and building technologies, but they are all too often unable to find or understand what relevant information may be available. This author does not pretend to be among the former, but has been among the latter for thirty years.

I am a student of the concrete experts–hopefully a worthy one, but certainly one who has been frustrated, as a practicing structural engineer, with the difficulties of translating the wealth of academic literature into practice. That is said not as a criticism–the academic foundation had to be laid–but by way of noting what prompted me to write this text. The use of fly ash in concrete, and particularly of high fly ash concrete (HFAC), is too great a benefit to the industry, to building owners, and to society as a whole to be ignored. This book was written in the simple hope of facilitating acceptance and usage of HFAC around the world.

I am indebted to innumerable people who have patiently educated me about fly ash in concrete, but more importantly about the positive benefits of higher fly ash usage for society. First and foremost are the two individuals to whom this work is dedicated: Dr. V. M. Malhotra of the Canada Centre for Mineral and Energy Technology (CANMET) in Ottawa, Canada, and especially my friend and mentor P. K. Mehta, Emeritus Professor of Civil Engineering at the University of California, Berkeley. Together, they have been central in bringing the issues of sustainability to the attention of the concrete industry. You will be hard-pressed to find any paper or research related to fly ash in concrete that does not reference either or both of these great men's works, usually many times. Many thanks also go to Tom Fox, Doug Yeggy, Jim Johnson, and Joe Seay of Headwaters, Inc.; Mason Walters, SE, of Forell-Elsesser Engineers; Scott Shell of Esherick, Holmsey, Dodge & Davis (EHDD) Architects; Burt Lockwood of Central ReadyMix; Michael Curran, Chris Avant, and Deva Rajan of Canyon Construction; Brian Adams of Degussa (Master Builders); Scot Horst of Horst, Inc. and the Athena Institute; and Jon Asselanis and Dushyant Manmohan of AME Testing Laboratories. As is the case with any work of science or engineering, there are also many authors, both known and unknown, current and ancient, whose research in some way underlies this text; even if not mentioned here, their role is acknowledged and appreciated.

Each and all, from Archimedes and Newton to Mehta and Malhotra, are thanked for their help, and must be held above reproach for any mistakes in the text which would be entirely my own.

Bruce King
July 2005
Sausalito, California

A Note About Numbers and Graphics

This is not an academic paper; it is a guidebook. A number of graphs appear in the pages that follow, each derived from one or several sources. They are presented to convey *tendencies* and *concepts,* not quantities. The specific shape of each curve will vary with the many factors involved, such as type of cement, type and percentage replacement of fly ash, conditions of curing, and so forth. We want to get the *ideas* across; if you want more specific information, there's plenty available in the references listed in the back of this book. We also want to emphasize, over and over, that sooner or later you will need to design your *own* mix with *your* aggregates, *your* cement, and *your* fly ash, and find out for yourself how it mixes, places, finishes, and performs. As anyone in the concrete industry knows, you cannot just take someone else's mix design from another region, with different materials, climate, requirements, and constraints, and expect it to suit yours. Use this book as a guide to designing and *testing* the fly ash mix that works best for you and your project circumstances.

Also: apologies to readers more familiar with the metric system of measurement. Most of the numbers that *do* exist in the text use our quirky imperial units of inches, pounds, yards, and such, but to keep things as simple as possible we decided not to clutter the book with bracketed translations. We leave that to you to do where needed, and trust it will present no problem.

MONTEREY BAY AQUARIUM
MONTEREY, CALIFORNIA,
1985

*HFAC used to protect
exposed concrete structure
from sea water and salt air*

Ninety percent of this game is half mental.

— Leo Durocher

INTRODUCTION

Coal fly ash is an abundant industrial waste product that happens to be high in reactive silica, and thus an excellent *pozzolan* (which we'll define in Chapter 2). For this simple reason it is rapidly becoming a common ingredient in concrete all over the world; it is already present to some degree in half the concrete poured in the US. The reasons for this are many, as will be described in the pages to follow. Of particular interest to the industry is the idea of not just adding fly ash to known concrete mixes, but using large quantities to *replace* 30%, 50%, or more of the portland cement–the glue–in a concrete mix. Most of the reasons for using fly ash in *any* proportion are practical, such as increasing strength and durability, decreasing heat of hydration, and decreasing permeability. Those reasons alone make the idea of high fly ash concrete (HFAC) worth considering, but there are many global economic, health, and environmental concerns that make HFAC even more attractive and compelling.

The use of fly ash as a performance-enhancing ingredient in concrete is one of the most outstanding examples of *industrial ecology*–i.e., making effective use of waste resources, and ultimately eliminating the concept of waste altogether. In fact, given the huge (and growing) volume of concrete production worldwide, the potential for effectively using fly ash (and other common industrial by-products) makes it one of the key components of a global industrial ecology.

There is, not surprisingly, disagreement among fly ash experts. Some will argue for higher or lower portions of fly ash than you will find presented in this book. The term HFAC is generally interpreted as referring to concrete in which fly ash replaces about 50% of the cement. However, in some cases 40% or 10% will be more appropriate, and in others 100% replacement is possible. Some experts will argue that 30% replacement is the *most* one should ever use, while others argue that you won't get the greatest benefits of HFAC *until* you get up to or over 40% or 50% replacement. The right figure for *your* project in *your* location will depend on many things, as will be reviewed in the pages to come.

This book is not an academic treatise. It will provide a cursory look at the history, economics, and performance effects of fly ash in concrete, but mainly is intended to provide practical guidelines for those who want to use it. Here you will find some basic do's and don'ts for ready-mix suppliers, concrete contractors, engineers, and others involved in concrete construction. Those who want more detailed material on any subject—and there's plenty available—can find references in the back of this book. Using HFAC is not rocket science, but neither is it obvious or intuitive. Now, however, you can now learn from the experience of others before using it yourself.

How much fly ash makes concrete "green"?

The short answer is: *any* fly ash in the mix as replacement for cement, up to the limits discussed in this text, will make for better concrete and reduce the atmospheric carbon load associated with cement production. In many areas, 15% to 20% addition or replacement is already standard practice, and is mandated by such governmental agencies as the California Department of Transportation (CALTRANS). The contention here is that, in most applications, about 50% replacement results in concrete that is better for the builder, for the building owner, and for the planet.

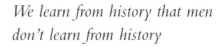

*We learn from history that men
don't learn from history*

– George Bernard Shaw

A SHORT HISTORY OF FLY ASH AND POZZOLANS IN CONCRETE

Fly ash in concrete is nothing new. Seventy years ago, the US Bureau of Reclamation made use of natural pozzolans (see chapter 2 for a definition of "pozzolans") and fly ash in the construction of the big dams of the American west, primarily to control heat of hydration. The great architect Louis Kahn used fly ash in concrete for the Salk Institute, mainly to lighten its color. Today, growing numbers of major structural concrete projects are being built in Canada and the United States using high volumes of fly ash to increase strength, workability, and durability.

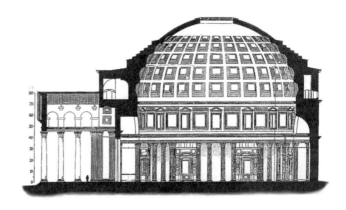

**THE PANTHEON
ROME, ITALY, 180 AD**

Lime plaster mixed with pozzolanic sand and a bare minimum of water (just enough so that the mixture could be moved around onsite in wicker baskets without leaking) was rammed between the masonry facing walls to make an extremely durable concrete.

However, the technology for using pozzolans could be said to go back thousands of years, far predating the invention of portland cement in the early 1800s or the coal-fired power plants that generate fly ash. Lime plasters—the precursors to both Roman and modern concrete—date as far back as 2500 BC in India, Mesopotamia, China, and the Mediterranean. No one knows for certain, of course, how things started, but probably a large bonfire encircled by limestone rocks reached a high enough temperature to calcine the limestone, turning it unexpectedly into quicklime. Soon enough, rain falling on the quicklime would cause it to hiss, spit, and heat up. Someone eventually discovered that the resulting material could be ground up, mixed with more water, and applied to earthen walls in a paste that hardened to a much greater density and durability than any manmade thing previously known. Lime plaster was born, and concrete would eventually follow.

The next step in the development of concrete was to improve the lime by adding reactive silica. The ancients found that ground-up pottery shards (calcined clay—the precursor of the modern pozzolan *metakaolin*), when mixed with lime, created a much harder plaster that would even cure under water. Later, the Romans were able to produce the same effect by using certain volcanic soils from the region of Pozzuoli, Italy—hence the term *pozzolans*. The famous Roman concrete which survives to this day is a mixture of lime plaster and pozzolanic soil. In *The Ten Books of Architecture,*

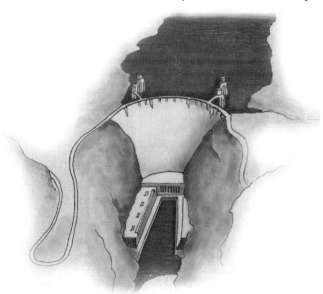

Vitruvius explained this in terms of the (then-known) primordial elements of earth, water, fire, and air. Nowadays, we explain Roman concrete by saying that hydrated lime reacted with amorphous silica in the pozzolanic soils to provide the "glue" for the concrete. We describe the effects of adding fly ash to portland cement in a similar way: hydrated lime (remaining from the hydration of portland cement) combines with the reactive silica in fly ash to better hold the concrete together. Of course, it's not all that simple, but the approximation will get us started.

**HOOVER DAM
NEVADA / ARIZONA 1939**

Despite the relatively poor quality of ash available at the time, fly ash and natural pozzolans were used to control the heat of concrete hydration when Hoover Dam was poured— an extremely important consideration in massive concrete pours, then as it is now.

If we are going to produce structures that have a service life of at least 100 years, HFA concrete and concrete with high volumes of other pozzolans such as slag, rice hull ash and metakaolin, will be the concrete of choice. Straight portland cement concrete is being replaced by a superior concrete product.

Burt Lockwood
Central Concrete Supply
Manager, Technical Services

2

*I'll play it for you first
and tell you what it is later.*

– Miles Davis

WHAT IS FLY ASH?
WHAT ARE POZZOLANS?

Fly ash comes from coal, used for fuel in most electrical power plants worldwide. Coal is rarely found in the earth without a few other minerals and rocks present; there is always some clay, shale, limestone, feldspar, and/or other trace minerals. Those incombustible materials are ground up with the coal and fuse during combustion. Ultimately they either settle to the bottom of the furnace as *bottom ash* or fuse and rise with the heated air as microscopic glass beads, thus to be called *fly ash*. Fly ash is simply the dust collected from the smokestacks. To the concrete industry, it is but one of a broader class of materials called *pozzolans*, or *mineral admixtures*, which are primarily characterized by high quantities of reactive silica. Fly ash also contains lesser amounts of iron, alumina, calcium, magnesium, sulfur, potassium, and sodium, often in oxidized forms; it is less dense than cement, with a specific gravity of 1.9 to 2.8, as contrasted with 3.15 for cement.

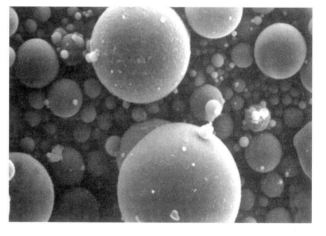

FLY ASH PARTICLES UNDER SCANNING ELECTRON MICROSCOPE.

Unlike cement and other pozzolans, fly ash particles are spherical, like ball bearings. Along with their electrostatic properties that keep cement particles from clumping, and their ability to fill micropores, this is why fly ash reduces water demand in concrete mixes.

Image courtesy of Headwaters Resources

What are pozzolans?

First, the technical definition: the American Society for Testing and Materials (ASTM) standard C618 says: *a **pozzolan** is a siliceous or siliceous and aluminous material, which in itself possesses little or no cementitious value but which will, in finely divided form and in the presence of moisture, chemically react with calcium hydroxide at ordinary temperatures to form compounds possessing cementing properties.*

There are all sorts of pozzolans currently available in the marketplace. Each can be characterized by its **source**:

- mined directly from the earth, such as diatomaceous earth and some volcanic tuffs

- manufactured, such as calcined clay (metakaolin)

- retrieved as industrial by-products, such as slag, fly ash, and silica fume (more of these are being discovered and tried every year)

- others, such as rice hull ash (the burned and ground hulls from rice kernels)

A. Pozzolans defined by source and standards organizations

The American Society for Testing and Materials' Standard ASTM C618 places all pozzolans in one of three categories:

Class N   Natural pozzolans such as volcanic tuffs and pumicite (what the Romans used), opaline cherts and shales, and diatomaceous earth, as well as calcined (fired) materials such as calcined kaolin clays (*Metakaolin*).

Class C   Fly ash characterized mainly, and some would say mistakenly, by a calcium oxide (CaO) content above 10%. Some say that that the class of fly ash should be defined more accurately by the sum of the oxides of silica, alumina, and iron.

Class F   Most coal sources in the US produce class F fly ash. The CaO content of Class F fly ash is usually below 16-18%, and often well under 10%. The CaO content, if high enough, makes the fly ash self-cementing, but also makes it less resistant to alkali-silica reaction (ASR) and to sulfate attack.

ASTM has separate standards for other relatively common pozzolans, such as ground granulated blast furnace slag (GGBFS)–ASTM C989, and silica fume–ASTM C1240. (It bears mentioning that the American Concrete Institute's ACI 318, and most building codes, limit the amount of fly ash in concrete to 25% of cementitious materials where the concrete will be exposed to deicing salts. This constraint is often misunderstood as applying to *all* concrete, when in fact it is probably unduly conservative even as written, as the general quality of fly ash in the marketplace has increased substantially since that standard was developed. The technology of concrete production has also improved to allow the use of greater percentages in concrete while maintaining or increasing durability.)

ASTM C618 and the other national standards for fly ash are all slightly different, carefully defining fly ash in terms of chemical and physical properties, moisture content, loss on ignition, and/or particle size distribution. In comparing all of these against each other and against laboratory and field experience, experts have concluded that many of the requirements are irrelevant to the performance of fly ash in concrete. They propose a simplified standard for all pozzolans that sets a combination of prescriptive and performance standards for the properties that matter:

1. **Loss on Ignition (LOI)** The unburned carbon residue on the surface of or commingled with fly ash particles. Generally, though not always, the higher the LOI the lower the Strength Activity Index (SAI—see below), and the more difficult it is to attain air entrainment. ASTM C618 and many other standards set an upper boundary of 6%, which is widely regarded as reasonable, and which is easily met by most North American fly ashes.

2. **Particle Size** The typical fly ash particle is a microscopic sphere anywhere from 1 to 100 microns in diameter (a micron is one thousandth of a millimeter; a millimeter is four hundredths of an inch); its particle size distribution is much like that of portland cement. The smaller particles, less than 10 microns in diameter, do most of the pozzolanic work, and are thus what you want. A typical fly ash has about 40% of its particles in this range, with the average particle being about 20 microns in diameter. Particles over 45 microns in diameter are less useful for pozzolanic activity, so this proposed but controversial standard sets a limit at 20% of particles above this size (ASTM C618 currently limits it to 34%). Some argue that an even distribution of ash particle sizes makes for a beneficial packing effect, just as on a larger scale a well-designed gradation from sand to small aggregate to large aggregate makes for better concrete. However, many reports based on field experience contradict these general guidelines; there is as yet no clear way to correlate an ash's effectiveness with its particle size gradation.

3. **Strength Activity Index (SAI)** This is, in concept, a performance standard that demonstrates the relative effectiveness of a pozzolan. Many SAI tests have been proposed, but as yet there is no universally accepted method. It usually amounts to making carefully defined and cured batches of ordinary portland cement concrete and portland/pozzolan concrete—usually as mortar cubes—then measuring and comparing the pozzolan's effect on strength and other important properties at various ages.

B. Pozzolans defined by reactivity and availability

Pozzolans can also be characterized by their pozzolanic **reactivity**, or the degree to which they affect the quality of the concrete.

1. **Cementitious and highly active pozzolans.** When a pozzolan contains a fair amount of calcium, it will be cementitious by itself, requiring only water to hydrate and harden. Examples include:

COAL-FIRED POWER PLANT – A SYNTHETIC POZZOLAN FACTORY

Most of the world's electricity, now and for the foreseeable future, comes from burning coal. As long as we're getting power that way, we can and should use the by-product—fly ash—to reduce air pollution and make better concrete. If the ash flies out the smokestack, it becomes smog and causes respiratory illness; if it's collected and used properly, it provides better concrete.

> **Ground granulated blast furnace slag (GGBFS, aka "slag"):** A by-product of the steel industry, GGBFS requires a fair amount of processing to become a useful pozzolan, but it is highly valued and is already being used in concrete around the world as a cement supplement and replacement. It is a highly effective pozzolan, both from the standpoint of concrete quality and in terms of environmental impact, deserving the promotion it is beginning to get. But there simply isn't enough GGBFS to have the widespread impact that higher usage of fly ash can have. Worldwide annual production of slag is 22 million tons, while that of fly ash is about 300 million tons. In North America, annual production of slag is about 3 million tons, while that of fly ash is about 60 million tons. (For perspective: the world uses about 1.6 billion tons of portland cement annually.)

> **Class C (high-calcium) fly ash:** Class C ashes, like fly ashes in general, require no processing (e.g., grinding) to be useful as pozzolans. Some concretes have been made with class C ashes (or slag) using no portland cement at all.

2. **Highly active pozzolans.** When a pozzolan has a very high percentage of reactive silica particles in the very small size range (well below ten microns), it is then proportionately more reactive with the hydration products of cement. There are three primary examples:

Silica fume: A by-product of the silicon industry, silica fume consists entirely of extremely small (⅒ micron) reactive silica particles, and has been used for decades as a key ingredient of very high-strength concrete. Because it is such a fine powder (and a health hazard if inhaled, like most pozzolans and cement), it is difficult and expensive to work with. The very small particle size also requires the use of superplasticizers to provide workability without increasing water content.

Rice hull ash (RHA): When rice is milled, the papery hulls (or husks) covering the grain are removed. The world produces about 60 million tons of rice hulls annually, which are essentially pure silica; many ideas have been proposed or tried for making effective use of them. One such idea is to burn them in electrical cogeneration power plants, of which at least a half dozen now operate in North America. If the hulls are burned at a controlled low temperature—not always the case at those power plants—the resulting ash is amorphous, that is noncrystalline. The amorphous ashes, when finely ground in a ball mill, become highly reactive pozzolans. Over the past few decades, various efforts to bring RHA to market, both commercial and UN-sponsored, have not met with success. As a result, RHA is not at present readily available.

MOUNT ST. HELENS— A NATURAL POZZOLAN PLANT

Certain types of volcanic eruptions will deposit tuffaceous soils (like the ones the Romans discovered in Pozzuoli, Italy) that are natural pozzolans. Such deposits can be found all over the world.

Metakaolin: Pure kaolin clays are heated (calcined) and ground to produce the commercial product now readily available. This particular pozzolan has deep historical roots, in that the ancients ground up their pottery shards and mixed the resulting powder with lime plasters to get a much harder plaster—essentially, a cement plaster. Several versions of metakaolin are now commercially available under different product names.

3. **Normal pozzolans.** Pozzolans containing a relatively low amount of calcium, thus requiring cement hydration products to react with for hardened compounds. Examples include:

Class F (low-calcium) fly ash: A by-product of most coal-fired power plants in North America that burn anthracite or bituminous coal; generally the most ubiquitous type of ash available worldwide.

Natural pozzolans: Naturally occurring minerals as previously defined; they typically require grinding to be useful in concrete.

4. **Weak pozzolans.** This is a broad category of materials with pozzolanic properties that are not highly reactive for any of a number of reasons, such as a low reactive silica content or rough or crystalline particle texture.

Industrial by-products: Bottom ash, various metal slags, field-burnt rice hull ash, thermally treated wood and paper residue, thermally treated municipal waste, ground brick and pottery waste, and more. At present, all waste and ash materials that are available in any particular quantity and that show any promise either have been or are being investigated for their beneficial use in concrete.

Natural materials: Many types of clay. The use of clay as a binder is the key to most traditional and modern forms of earthen construction. Combining clay with modest quantities of lime or portland cement, and the material properties of the resulting compounds, is a subject of much modern research geared toward affordable and environmentally-friendly construction. That subject is large enough for another entire book, but bears at least mentioning here.

It is worth noting a couple of things about the fly ash marketplace as of this writing (early 2005):

1. Most fly ashes available in Europe and North America meet ASTM C618 criteria, and are readily useable and effective in concrete. However, most readily *accessible* ashes are already in the marketplace, and often in short supply. Plenty of ash is being generated, but it doesn't all get to market due to lack of economical access—typically meaning that there's no proximate rail line.

2. At present, there is pressure on the coal-fired power industry to reduce mercury, nitrous oxide (NO_x), sulphurous oxide (SO_x) and other polluting emissions. There is also pressure to combine pulverized coal with other fuels (e.g., municipal, wood, and animal wastes) to feed the flames in a cogeneration burning process. In such cases, reducing air pollution can sometimes reduce the effectiveness of fly ashes for use in concrete. Many studies have examined the effects

of pollution controls and cogeneration processes on the utility of fly ash (see selected articles from the references for more specific information). Amending and improving such affected ashes for use in concrete, called *beneficiation*, is a subject of increasing and fruitful study around the world.

PURDY'S WHARF RETAIL CENTER,
HALIFAX, NOVA SCOTIA, 1988

The first use of HFAC (50% replacement of cement) in structural concrete for buildings

Researchers have already shed much darkness on this subject, and if they continue their efforts we shall soon know nothing at all.

— Mark Twain

HOW DO FLY ASH AND POZZOLANS AFFECT CONCRETE?

When the portland cement in ordinary concrete hydrates—in other words, after you've added water—compounds of calcium, silica, and alumina (calcium silicates, abbreviated below as "CS") react with the water (abbreviated below as "H") to create a gel of calcium silicate hydrate (CSH). CSH is the glue that holds everything together and gives concrete its strength and durability. Unfortunately, a lot of the portland cement—often nearly half—in most concrete isn't fated to become CSH, but instead becomes hydrated lime, or calcium hydroxide (CH). That CH tends to show up as brittle crystals that gather on the surface of aggregate particles and rebar, making for a weakened matrix (see the transition zone illustration on next page).

If, however, you add a source of additional reactive silica (e.g., a pozzolan, such as fly ash), it will react with that calcium hydroxide in the presence of moisture to become more CSH—glue. In effect, the fly ash takes the weakest link in the chain, CH, and turns it into the strongest link in the chain, CSH. Like this:

THE BASIC POZZOLANIC REACTION— HOW FLY ASH MAKES FOR BETTER CONCRETE

Is it actually more complicated than this? Of course it is—vastly more complicated. But this will do for now. If you want to know more, see the reference material.

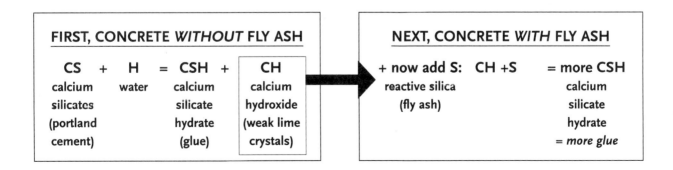

FIRST, CONCRETE *WITHOUT* FLY ASH

CS	+	H	=	CSH	+	CH
calcium silicates (portland cement)		water		calcium silicate hydrate (glue)		calcium hydroxide (weak lime crystals)

NEXT, CONCRETE *WITH* FLY ASH

+ now add S: CH +S   = more CSH
reactive silica
(fly ash)

calcium
silicate
hydrate
= more glue

THE TRANSITION ZONE

Bleed water rich in CH rises, some reaching the surface, but much collecting around and under each piece of aggregate and rebar. This makes for a weak zone of brittle crystals between the aggregate surface and the surrounding matrix of strong cement paste. As the bleed water rises, it also makes connections between transition zones, leading to a network of microcracks that weakens the concrete and leaves it vulnerable to water intrusion. The presence of reactive fly ash counters this effect, both by packing the pores with fine ash particles and by reacting with the lime in the water to form more glue (CSH).

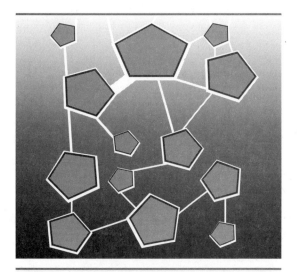

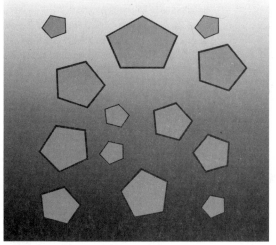

The calcium hydroxide (CH) that results from cement hydration tends to collect in the bleed water trapped under and around rebar and particles of sand and gravel— the so-called "wall effect." Eventually the CH dries, primarily in the form of weak, brittle microcrystals. To the extent that this happens—as it typically does in most concrete—the concrete's strength goes down and its permeability goes up. The same is then true, on a larger scale, of your structure.

Now add some reactive silica (S)—such as fly ash. If you proportion the ingredients right, and keep things moist, two good things happen:

1. the fine fly ash particles pack the voids between cement and aggregate particles, making it much harder for the bleed water to move around or form pockets and cracks, and

2. the silica reacts over time with the calcium hydroxide to make more glue: CH+S = CSH. Instead of a weak transition zone, you have a strong one; instead of high permeability resulting from a three-dimensional network of microcracks, you have impermeability. Instead of a little bit of glue holding things together, you have a lot of glue.

In a simplified nutshell, that's it.

A. Effects of fly ash on fresh concrete

1. Reduced water demand

Fly ash has been described as the "poor man's superplasticizer" because it can reduce water demand and increase workability and pumpability. There are at least three reasons for this:

1. the tiny particles of ash help pack voids between cement particles,

2. fly ash particles are spherically shaped, acting like ball bearings, and

3. probably most important, the ash particles have an electrostatic effect on cement particles that keeps them from clumping (flocculating)—a process that gums up the fresh concrete.

All of this gives fly ash an advantage over other pozzolans, almost all of which tend to increase water demand in fresh concrete. Note, however, that poor-quality ashes—with coarse particle sizes or high levels of unburned carbon—will usually not have this effect, and may even reverse it (see illustration). Such ashes are now rare in North America due to advanced technologies in the power plants, and most ashes in the marketplace are well-suited for concrete.

2. Reduced bleed water

The incorporation of 15% to 60% of quality fly ash will lower the water demand, so there will be less or no bleed (excess) water appearing on the surface of slabs and other pours—and a proportionately greater need to protect surfaces from premature drying. (See Chapter 5 on Construction Considerations for more about

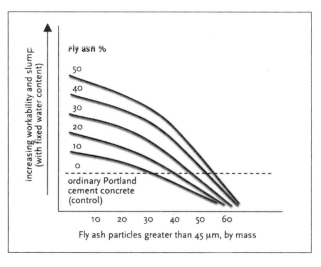

EFFECTS OF FLY ASH ON WATER DEMAND

Notice two things: with fine-grained fly ash, greater ash content in the concrete means greater slump. BUT as the ash becomes coarser (percentage of particles about 45 microns in size, which is big enough to feel gritty between the fingers), the effect diminishes and even reverses.

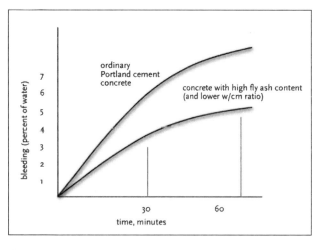

EFFECTS OF FLY ASH ON BLEED WATER

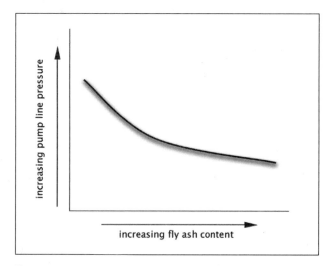

EFFECT OF FLY ASH CONTENT ON PUMPABILITY

Fly ash lubricates the fresh concrete in several ways, reducing wear on pumps and facilitating placement in the formwork.

Ordinary Portland cement concrete slump

Same mix with 20% fly ash replacement of cement

Images courtesy of Headwaters Resources

this.) The *rate* at which bleed water rises is also a reduced, so caution is needed to avoid finishing a slab before it's really ready; premature finishing can be followed by a rise in bleed water and consequent weakening of the surface.

3. Increased workability and pumpability

Laboratory studies and field experience indicate that HFAC is easier to pump and work than its conventional concrete counterpart, all other things being equal. This makes it easier on workers and pumps, and easier to consolidate and get into congested or complex formwork without the need for excessive vibrating, and without segregation or pocketing.

4. Continuing slump

When subjected to the standard cone test, HFAC will often show a certain slump, only to gain an additional inch or two after some time has passed. The material remains cohesive, but simply continues settling longer than its conventional concrete counterpart.

B. Effects of fly ash on plastic concrete

1. Extended set times

Initial and final set will be slower by an hour or two in a typical HFAC if the mix is not adjusted to counter this effect. In some cases, such as cool weather or misuse of chemical admixtures, set can be extended as long as overnight. The fact that fly ash provides greater early-age extensibility can be an advantage, as the concrete mass remains more ductile to redistribute forces and reduce plastic cracking.

2. Reduced heat of hydration

Portland cement gives off heat as it hydrates, especially in the first few days after pouring. In a massive concrete pour, the subsequent surface cooling (relative to the still-warm core) can lead to differential thermal-shrinkage cracking. If you reduce the amount of cement in the mix by replacing it with fly ash, the heat of hydration is reduced and you will have fewer thermal shrinkage cracks. (That is why some of the first uses of high volumes of fly ash in concrete were in dams—purely to reduce thermal cracking.) The fact that fly ash generally retards the rate of strength gain is, in this case, an advantage; the concrete mass remains relatively plastic as it changes size with temperature, and therefore cracks less. A four-foot-thick unreinforced slab, 60 by 120 feet in plan, was poured a few years ago in Hawai'i using 60% fly ash replacement (mix number 5 in appendix); to date, it shows no cracking at all (see "pouring Iraivan slab" illustration in chapter 5). In cool- or cold-weather concrete work, this same effect

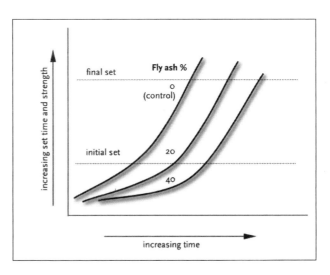

EFFECTS OF FLY ASH CONTENT ON SET TIME

Generally, increasing the amount of fly ash will delay initial and final set times, simply because there is less cement to give the mix its early "kick". (See chapter 5 for ways to accelerate the set.)

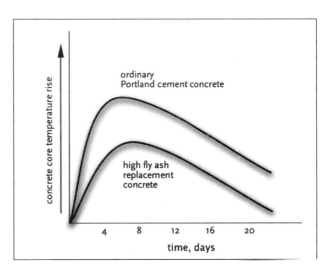

EFFECTS OF FLY ASH ON HEAT OF HYDRATION

can work against you, as it is more difficult to keep the concrete mass warm enough to insure proper hydration of the cement (see "cold-weather concrete placement" in Chapter 5).

Thermal cracking is not significant for a lot of concrete work, but studies have shown that any concrete pour with a smallest dimension of two or three feet can experience enough thermal change to cause cracking. Remember, the problem is not the heating up or cooling down of the concrete mass—generally, you *want* it quite warm for the first few days—but *differential* heating or cooling as the material hydrates in the critical first days. You don't want the surface temperatures to be different than the core, and the more the core heats up the more likely it is that there will be a difference.

3. Reduced plastic shrinkage cracking

The loss of water in the early stages of concrete's life is the main thing that causes the concrete volume to plastically shrink. If the mass is restrained in any way—as it almost always is by rebar, formwork, or the ground under a slab—then that shrinkage causes cracking. In a well-blended HFAC mix, there is less water and thus less volume change during the plastic phase.

C. Effects of fly ash on hardened concrete

1. Slower rate of strength gain

Increasing amounts of fly ash as cement replacement will generally slow the rate of strength gain. This tendency is less pronounced with class C ashes, and less pronounced when coarse aggregates are both increased and optimally graded. Slower rate of strength gain may or may not matter, as most concrete (e.g., foundations, columns, and slabs on grade) doesn't need to reach its design strength for at least two or three months after pouring. Flexural strength and Modulus of Elasticity are generally higher than for conventional concrete, depending on many factors.

2. Reduced permeability

All the elements of the pozzolanic reaction described earlier in this chapter—reduced cracking, a strengthened transition zone, particle packing of voids, and deflocculation of cement particles—contribute to reduced permeability. Increasing and grading coarse aggregates also lowers water demand through reduced aggregate surface area, further reducing permeability through reduction of transition zones.

3. Reduced drying shrinkage

As the illustration shows, drying shrinkage increases with cement and/or water content. Field experience has demonstrated that replacing cement with fly ash reduces shrinkage even when using aggregate

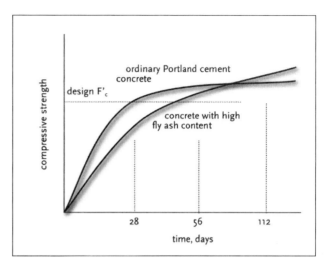

EFFECTS OF FLY ASH ON COMPRESSIVE STRENGTH

Generally, increasing the amount of fly ash will slow the initial strength gain. However, high fly ash concrete will typically meet strength requirements at 56 days and keep gaining appreciable strength as the pozzolanic reaction continues. Initial strength gain can be increased when necessary by using accelerating admixtures, type III (high early strength) cement, a high-grade pozzolan such as silica fume or rice hull ash, moist/hot curing, or some combination of these and other tricks.

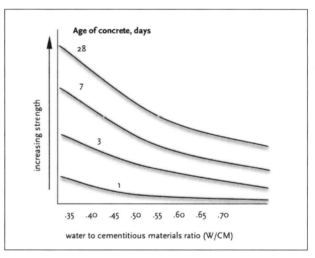

EFFECTS OF WATER CONTENT ON STRENGTH

This isn't complicated. The more water in your concrete, the lower the quality at every age. Fly ash reduces the need for adding water to attain workability. If you want good concrete, control the water in the mix from batching to transport to placing and curing.

3

HOW DO FLY ASH AND POZZOLANS AFFECT CONCRETE?

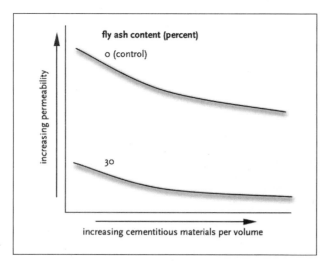

EFFECTS OF FLY ASH ON PERMEABILITY

The effect is dramatic. A well-designed, well-cured HFAC will be substantially less permeable than its conventional concrete counterpart, making it more durable, more resistant to rebar corrosion and chemical attack, and (if class F ash) more resistant to sulfate attack and alkali-silica reaction.

This reduced permeability also means there will be less efflorescence (calcium carbonate – the hard white mineral that slowly accretes on the surface of concrete and masonry), both because there is less cement to act as fuel, and because water cannot as easily leach out the free calcium to carbonate in the air.

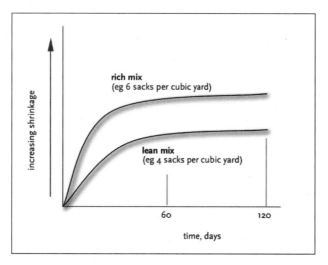

EFFECTS OF CEMENT CONTENT ON SHRINKAGE

Shrinkage in any concrete increases primarily with cement content and water content. Reduce either or both, and you reduce shrinkage.

prone to high shrinkage. By lowering the water content, shrinkage is further reduced.

4. Resistance to scaling from deicing salts

Early tests on the scaling resistance to deicing salts of concretes containing high proportions of fly ash and other pozzolans showed very poor results. This is probably why many building codes only address and limit the amount of fly ash in concrete *when in the presence of deicing salts.* By contrast, many field tests of actual sidewalk sections, using high fly ash replacement and exposed to deicing salts and repeated freeze-thaw cycles, have shown good results. As of this writing, the picture is still unclear. Researchers have speculated that the discrepancy appears because ASTM test C672 is in some way excessively conservative, or at least not representative of actual conditions. Testing has shown that the use of curing compounds is beneficial, and that finishing methods can influence the concrete durability. If you are contemplating HFAC work in this category, you are urged to get the most up-to-date information regarding resistance to deicing salts; an excellent resource is www.ecosmart.com.

GAP HEADQUARTERS
SAN FRANCISCO, CALIFORNIA, 2001

*HFAC used to resist seawater infiltration in
subgrade parking and foundations and to obtain
LEED credits. The concrete is still completely
uncracked as of this writing.*

My experience in battle is that plans are useless but planning is essential.

– Dwight Eisenhower

DESIGN CONSIDERATIONS

A. Get the whole team on board

Unless you happen to operate in an area where HFAC has become common, you will have to be sure that every stakeholder in the construction process is educated and aware of the ramifications, potential problems, and benefits of its use. The project owner, the design team (architect and structural engineer), and the construction team (general contractor, concrete subcontractor, ready-mix supplier, forming and finishing crews, and testing lab) all need to know what HFAC will mean to them and be given a chance to become comfortable with it. This is not easy on government and open-bid jobs, in which cases the drawings and specifications must be particularly clear and emphatic in pointing out those specific job requirements that are in any way unusual. Spell out a preconstruction testing program and timeline, if needed, and establish criteria for acceptance and rejection. Define the quality-control program during construction (see next section).

Listen to each party's concerns and suggestions. As is universally true in construction, a single person with doubts or resistance to the plan can make problems for the entire team. Conversely, good suggestions can come from anyone and deserve consideration. In one famously successful HFAC project, the admixture supplier was

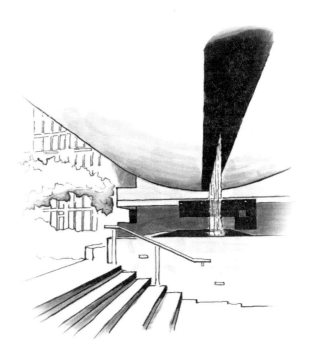

THE "WATERFALL BUILDING," VANCOUVER, BC, 2001

HFAC used for greater flowability in special concrete forms, lighter color as exposed concrete, and LEED credits

given free license to stand at the pump and add superplasticizer if and as he saw fit; his expertise and experience were recognized and accepted, and the result was outstanding concrete.

B. Call for the concrete performance you really need

A hundred years ago, someone noticed that concrete will typically attain about 80% of its ultimate strength in a month. Ever since then, engineers have habitually specified required concrete compressive strength (F'_c) at 28 days. That number is universally used in the industry as the benchmark for quality control in the field and for inferring other design properties of the concrete (e.g., shear strength and elastic modulus).

As noted in the previous chapter, HFAC is initially somewhat slower to gain strength than conventional concrete. But it will continue to gain strength as the months go by, unlike conventional concrete. In other words, the strength of HFAC at 28 days may be only half its ultimate strength. In most cases, concrete doesn't need full strength for several months and project specifications can simply be changed to F'_c at 56 days. That simple change alone—radical notion though it may be to some—can save a bag or more of cement per cubic yard of concrete, because you've allowed the concrete (and the ready-mix supplier worried about his responsibility) enough time to gain the needed strength. In the specifications, define the construction-phase quality control program—especially if it differs from normal practices, such as basing acceptance on the 56-day compressive strength vs. the usual 28-day strength.

In designing the seismic retrofit of Barker Hall on the UC Berkeley campus—right next to the Hayward Seismic Fault—we looked for High Fly Ash Concrete to provide these benefits: better flowability and consolidation, low shrinkage, low heat of hydration, reduced cracking, lower permeability, better corrosion protection, and greater durability for longer life. In every respect, HFAC met or exceeded our expectations.

Mason Walters, SE
Principal
Forell / Elsesser Structural Engineers, Inc.

In some cases, however, benchmarking 56-day compressive strength isn't good enough. Some concrete *does* need to gain strength quickly, such as retaining walls slated for immediate backfilling, post-tensioned slabs, and overhead beams or overhead slabs whose formwork can't be left in place for long. In those cases, initial strength gain can be increased through the use of accelerating admixtures, type III (high early strength) cement, a high-grade pozzolan (such as silica fume or rice-hull ash), moist/hot curing, water-content reduction, or a combination of these and other tricks.

C. Design, mix, place, and test trial batches ahead of time
(the carpenter's axiom: measure twice, cut once)

Common sense and the building codes require that you pretest any new concrete mix that doesn't have a history of use in your area. As anyone in the concrete industry knows, you cannot just take someone else's mix design from another region—with different materials, climate, requirements, and constraints—and expect it to suit yours. Use this book (and the references in the back) as a guide to designing and testing the HFAC mix that works best for you and your project circumstances. Some sample mixes are described in Appendix A, in the hope of providing suggestions and a starting point. It can't be emphasized enough, though: design your *own* mix with *your* aggregates, *your* cement, *your* fly ash, and *your* admixtures to find out for yourself how it mixes, places, finishes, and performs. If the concrete is to be exposed, this will also give everyone a chance to see how it looks.

Some people in the concrete industry, who have come to describe HFAC as *high-performance* concrete, view portland cement itself as an admixture—albeit usually a crucial one. Concretes have been poured with cement contents as low as 20%, 10%, and even 0% by instead using cementitious-pozzolanic minerals, such as slag and class C fly ash. For that matter, the Romans made some of the most beautiful and durable concrete structures in the world, and they sure didn't have any portland cement. In other words, it's an open question as to what should or should not go into any particular concrete mix.

You may have guessed by now that it's important to keep a low ratio of water to cementitious materials (W/CM; in this case, CM = cement + fly ash) ; 0.45 is generally considered a reasonable starting point for mix design. With well-graded aggregates and a high-quality ash, you won't necessarily need to add water-reducing agents to attain the workability needed for your project. If you want a higher rate of strength gain, or for some other reason want to lower the W/CM ratio to below 0.40, you will need one or more water-reducing agents—and everyone involved will need to pay special attention to doing everything right. This is one

more reason to make trial mixes and see how they perform. Field experience has shown that slight changes in admixture proportions can have large effects on set time, slump and other properties of the concrete.

Where air entrainment is necessary, be aware that HFAC mixes often require higher dosages of air-entraining agents. Furthermore, at all ages, concrete strength decreases with increasing air content. Class C ashes, ashes with coarse particle sizes, and ashes with a high carbon content (LOI) are generally found to require a higher proportion of air-entrain-ing agent, but there are plenty of exceptions; each ash is unique.

Again, this is not easy on government and open-bid jobs, and may only be possible if the project schedule allows a few months ahead of any concrete pour to initiate a test program. If that is the case, in the job specifications call clearly for a prelimi-nary testing program, possibly even with tentative mix designs. If the benchmark is

> *We have found that HFAC is better concrete, easier to use, and less likely to crack. It makes our customers and engineers happy, so it makes us happy. It is not complicated or all that different than regular concrete. In fact, many of the basic principles required to place successful HFAC also apply to regu-lar concrete, such as keeping the water ratios low and implementing reason-able curing practices.*
>
> Deva Rajan
> Founder & Chairman
> Canyon Construction Company

to be F'_c at 56 days, as suggested, then the preliminary testing program can and should call for many cylinder breaks at 3, 7, 28, and 56 days. This gives all parties a clear look at how the mix will perform—a strength-development curve. With that in hand, the construction testing agency can cure and break cylinders at, say, 7 days so as to get an early check on performance; no one wants to wait 56 days to find out that something went wrong.

D. Use HFAC to counteract common problems

A well-designed, well-graded HFAC mix with minimal water content and proper curing is a *high-performance* concrete; it is stronger, tighter (against water infiltration), and therefore more durable. In particular, an abundance of evidence shows that HFAC can be used to lower the heat of hydration in mass concrete, increase resistance to corrosion and degradation caused by high-sulfate soils, reactive aggregates, salt air or water, or caustic chemicals (e.g., dairy plants, wineries, and gas stations). Where these and other environmental factors are present, you have all the more reason to use HFAC, and you should design your mix accordingly. Note, however, differences between class F and class C ashes; the latter may help accelerate early strength gain, but will sometimes diminish resistance to ASR (alkali-silica reaction) and sulfate corrosion, while adding to the heat of hydration. Once again, testing of the specific mix is essential to getting the desired properties.

E. Check for availability of fly ash—and expert help

In the San Francisco area, HFAC has become nearly routine to many engineers, builders, and concrete suppliers and contractors; it's no longer "new," and using it is no big deal. In most areas, however, that's not the case. Many ready-mix suppliers routinely stock and use fly ash in bulk. In other cases, you may have to special-order it in bulk, bagged, or intermixed as type IP cement in bags.

In the last few years, fly ash in North America has changed from being an abundant, inexpensive waste product into a highly desired commodity that is often in short supply. Globally, we produce plenty of fly ash, but too much of it still literally goes up in smoke or is not readily available to consumers via the only economical route—railway lines connecting to the power plant.

You may also want at least one person on the team who is familiar with HFAC, to address the many questions that come up. That person may be the concrete supplier, but will probably be either the local fly ash sales representative or a knowledgeable representative of one of the chemical admixture companies. (Almost all early work with HFAC involved high-range water-reducing admixtures, so the purveyors of those products have been involved with the evolution of HFAC from the beginning.)

F. Pay attention during construction

You get what you *inspect*, not necessarily what you *expect*. Review procedures with the project team; watch for changes in the design, material supplies, personnel, or weather that might affect concrete work; and, especially, make sure that curing procedures are understood and followed by all. Thus Dwight Eisenhower's admonishment: *My experience in battle is that plans are useless, but planning is essential.* In life, as in construction, as with HFAC, things change whether we like it or not; be prepared to adapt.

G. Check for exposure to deicing salts

As discussed, the discrepancy between laboratory experiments and field experience leaves the picture a bit muddied: how much additional vulnerability to scaling, if any, does HFAC have when exposed to deicing salts? Study the reference material, in particular websites such as Ecosmart, for the most current research.

H. Evaluate conditions: *a rough guide to how easy or hard it may be to use HFAC in different applications*

1. Definitely use HFAC! *easy or obvious applications*

- drilled piers and caissons
- massive pours, such as dams, mat slabs, or roller-compacted concrete
- most poured footings in earth
- grouting of concrete block or block-type insulating concrete forms
- piers and walls exposed to seawater (because you'd be foolish not to have the added impermeability)
- exposed concrete (because HFAC is lighter-colored and flows into forms more smoothly)
- poured-in-place concrete walls and columns (because HFAC gives greater flowability and you don't need early strength)

2. Probably use HFAC

good applications, but think everything through, such as set time and curing

- retaining and basement walls (accelerate the rate of strength gain if needed)

- slabs on grade (if you can be sure to protect them from premature drying)

- shotcrete and gunite (if you can tarp it or otherwise insure a good cure)

3. Be careful!

easy-to-screw-up applications—usually when curing is difficult, or you need early strength

- slabs on grade in very hot, windy, or cold weather
  (unless you can really protect them)

- cold-weather concrete pours (sometimes you
  just need that cement to keep things warm)

- precast elements that require fast turnaround (removal from forms)

- elevated beams and slabs where formwork will be removed quickly

- tilt-up construction (can you develop strength
  quickly enough to handle lifting stresses?)

Having read all of the above, perhaps you can see why this book provides no "sample specifications"; there simply is no "one size fits all" document. Rather, the admonitions and suggestions can be used to amend a conventional concrete specification as needed.

**BARKER HALL
SEISMIC RETROFIT,
BERKELEY, CALIFORNIA,
2001**

HFAC used for seismic retrofit of multistory dormitory almost on top of the high-risk Hayward Fault, chosen primarily for added long-term strength and extra flowability within congested forms.

They say you can't do it,
but sometimes it doesn't always work.

– Casey Stengal

CONSTRUCTION CONSIDERATIONS

A. Controlling the water content

More than a few times in my career as an engineer, I have come to a job site the day after a concrete pour to find the contractor eagerly stripping form-work from walls because "the sun can then shine on it and dry it out and make it cure faster." The best word for this situation is "Ouch!"–both because the premature exposure to sun has the opposite, ie terrible, effect, and because an otherwise competent builder understands so little about a material he works with every day.

Place concrete, especially HFAC, with *no more water than is absolutely needed*. Then take every possible measure to keep that moisture in the concrete for at least the first few weeks; protect it like a newborn baby from sun, wind, and cold.

The two most common ways of wrecking concrete in those all-important first weeks are adding too much water, and/or not curing the concrete properly (in other words, not keeping the mix water in the concrete). This is even more true of HFAC, which works only when water content is minimized.

The following comments only apply if you heed the preceding advice.

In fact, if you don't plan to control water content and cure the concrete well, throw this book away; it will do you no good.

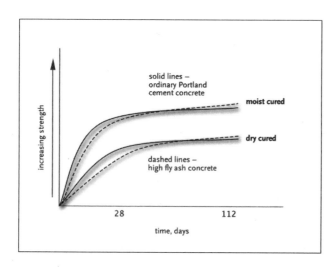

solid lines –
ordinary Portland
cement concrete

moist cured

increasing strength

dry cured

dashed lines –
high fly ash concrete

28   112

time, days

**EFFECTS OF CURING
CONDITIONS ON STRENGTH**

*With any concrete,
warm moist curing is ideal,
especially during the first
week. By contrast, exposure
to drying sun or wind can
radically decrease quality
and increase shrinkage
cracking. All of this is even
more applicable to HFAC,
mostly because the water
content starts out lower,
so less water can be "lost"
without causing problems.*

B. Longer set time

As was described earlier, increasing percentages of
fly ash (or water content) in the mix will retard set
times and rate of strength gain. Sometimes this
doesn't matter, as when walls can be left in their
forms for three days or a week. When it *does* matter, the rate of strength gain can be increased in a
number of ways–see chapter 4.

C. Slabs–special considerations
1. less or no bleed water

After pouring and floating an HFAC slab, there
will be little or no bleed water appearing on the surface–the traditional
gauge by which finishing crews know when to start finishing. Also, what
bleed water there is will take longer to rise, so a trial pour is essential to
give the crew a feel for how the concrete sets up and feels under the trow-
el. Premature finishing can trap bleed water, leading to surface spalling.
Some have reported a sticky quality to fresh slabs, affecting the way they
finish. Wooden bull floats work better than magnesium ones. Wait for final
finishing procedures until the concrete will support the weight of a work-
man with less than a one fourth inch indentation.

2. vulnerability to premature drying

Slabs have far more surface area than any other
kind of concrete pour, and so are that much
more susceptible to premature drying when
exposed to sun, wind, or even just warm, dry
air. Protecting freshly poured concrete from
drying is essential with any slab, but especially
so with HFAC. Depending on circumstances,
protective measures may include: pouring and
finishing at night, spraying the finished surface
as soon as possible with a liquid curing com-
pound (two coats are better than one!), and
covering the surface with plastic or
burlap/plastic tarps (with moistened burlap

layers facing down). Slabs that are partly in sunlight and partly in shade can show different initial set times, which affects the finishing schedule.

HFAC slabs on metal decking (e.g., in high-rise construction) give off less water vapor at both early and late stages because of their lower water content and denser particle structure. They have thus been successfully used to help avoid delamination of bonded flooring materials, a big problem in commercial construction.

3. vulnerability to shrinkage cracking

If carefully protected and cured, an HFAC slab will shrink and crack less than its conventional concrete counterpart. As was discussed, this is mainly due to the lowered cement and water content of the mix, but is also due to the slower set time; the slab remains somewhat plastic as it changes size in the first few days. Conversely, if an HFAC slab is *not* carefully cured, it can shrink, crack, and curl up at the edges even more because it remains longer in the plastic condition—the time during which concrete is most vulnerable to the many problems that result from premature drying. Be forewarned, and read item A of this chapter again.

4. staining and coloring

HFAC is generally slightly lighter than ordinary concrete, making it easier to get a color or finish that you want. However, the lower permeability of HFAC means that stains won't penetrate as deeply; this may or may not matter much, depending on the project conditions. Whether using stains or integral color, the need for preconstruction testing—including plenty of time for full curing—is all the more important so as to see ahead of time how your particular mix of ingredients and applications will work.

POURING AND FLOATING
THE MASS FOUNDATION
SLABS FOR THE IRAIVAN
TEMPLE, KAUAI, 2001

HFAC used in an unreinforced mat slab foundation for extreme durability—"built to last a thousand years" (no cracks at all in an unreinforced mat measuring 130 ft. x 60 ft. x 4 ft. thick).

D. Hot- and cold-weather concrete placement

Extreme weather conditions will affect any concrete work, and the first and primary guide is ACI's *Manual of Standard Practice*, including guidelines for hot-weather and cold-weather concrete work. Precautions for HFAC work are different as follows:

- in hot weather, the tendency to prematurely dry is exacerbated, and

- in cold weather—even relatively mild cold weather—the lower heat of hydration that makes HFAC preferable for mass pours can become a disadvantage. Concrete doesn't like to get too chilly while setting; if it does, the cement doesn't hydrate properly and the fly ash has fewer reaction products (CH) with which to develop additional strength. The heat generated by the hydration of cement is typically what keeps cold-weather concrete curing, along with insulated forms and tarps when needed. When contemplating HFAC in cold weather, extra insulation, heaters, hot mix water, or even just leaving more portland cement in the mix may be called for.

E. Formwork

HFAC can be slower to set up and have a higher slump than conventional concrete; it also has better workability that an equal-slump ordinary concrete. To the extent that this is true for your project, make allowances. Tall walls must have sturdier formwork to resist the additional liquid pressure, and must sometimes be sealed against leakage. If 2x dimensional lumber is used as formwork, as is common in residential construction, and it is to be left in place for a week to assist curing, then it will often end up "cupped" to the extent that it's no longer useable for framing.

For walls as low as four feet high, you might need to place the footings first, then form and pour the walls. Otherwise, if you try and place the footings and walls monolithically, HFAC will "boil" out of the wall forms from the footings. For high walls (over six feet), use of an accelerator with a compatible water-reducing agent will help insure an early set from lift to lift.

After placing HFAC for over five years, our concrete teams in the field tell us that they prefer it over regular concrete. They work closely with the batch plant and pumping operators on each pour to insure a smooth and successful placement every time. This new technology makes our men especially proud of our finished concrete work: fewer cracks (if any), low permeability that enhances durability, and strength-test results that are off the charts.

Deva Rajan
Founder & Chairman
Canyon Construction Company

F. Use of chemical admixtures

Concrete once consisted of gravel, sand, cement, and water. Period. Here and there, that may still be the case, but most modern concrete is a brew of those basic ingredients plus some combination of mineral and chemical admixtures added for various purposes, such as to increase slump, entrain air for freeze-thaw protection, and accelerate or retard setting and curing times.

Use of HFAC often—though by no means always—involves the use of normal, mid- or high-range water-reducing admixtures to lower the W/CM ratio and maintain workability. In cold climates, air entrainment is mandatory, and higher dosages are often necessary in HFAC to achieve the desired level of entrainment.

As with conventional concrete, learning how any combination of admixtures will affect your HFAC is very much a matter of trial and error. You simply have to cast test batches to see how the mix pours, finishes, sets, strengthens, and so on. Furthermore, notwithstanding all the smooth curves used in this book to illustrate various properties of HFAC, field experience shows that any concrete can be finicky in its behavior with varying amounts of admixtures. A little too much water-reducer can cause premature gelling, but too little (or too much of another kind) can *retard* the set. It depends very much on exactly which admixtures, dosages, and combinations are being used.

SHEARWALL REINFORCING FOR BARKER HALL SEISMIC RETROFIT

HFAC proved very useful for its greater flowability in forms that were both highly congested with rebar and conduit, and slated to be exposed concrete. There were substantially fewer pockmarks and voids than the contractor and engineer expected.

Photo courtesy of Forell-Elsesser Structural Engineers

Furthermore, when casting trial batches, keep an eye on scheduling. A test slab cast and finished in February can only tell you so much about how the pour will go in late August, and vice versa. Lab-produced initial set times are often a poor indicator of actual field performance. Pouring small samples in the field not only provides more relevant results, but it also gives crews a chance to work the mix.

Here are some rules of thumb for using admixtures based on field experience:
- Water-reducing agents should be dosed to the cement content not the cement + fly ash content.
- "Normal" water reducers should be used for mixes with less than 5″ of desired slump.
- "Mid-Range" water reducers should be used for mixes with a slump of 5″-8″; lower slump is possible, but slump retention may suffer (you may get early gelling).

- "High-Range" water reducers should only be used for mixes with a desired slump greater than 8"; lower slump can cause severe slump loss (early gelling).
- For HFAC, "Mid-Range" and "High-Range" water reducers are highly preferable; "Normals" can cause greatly extended set times in high-ash mixes. The new generation of polycarboxylate-based "super"-superplasticizers work well with fly ash, but as always you need to test each mix carefully. There are now water-reducing agents in the marketplace specifically tailored to HFAC, and these are generally preferable.
- If the job is to be constructed during cold weather, use hot water and, where possible, and an accelerator. Even mildly cool weather or the shade of trees and buildings can retard the set of slabs, as by definition you don't have as much cement content to heat up and jump-start the curing process.

There is no way to predict how different chemical admixtures will interact, so many trial batches may be required to get the right combination of cement, ash, aggregate gradation, water reducers, and other chemical admixtures. In some of the larger successful HFAC projects, the team literally tried dozens of formulas before settling on the one that worked best for the project needs. You may not have the luxury of running so extensive a preconstruction test program, but it remains true that, as with all concrete, you don't know what to expect with any given mix until you've tried it out in one way or another.

G. Aggregate gradation

Innumerable laboratory and field experiences have shown that well-designed "particle packing," both at the scale of cement and ash particles and at the scale of sand/pea gravel/large aggregate, will reduce water demand and make for much better concrete. Consider replacing some of the sand or large aggregate in a mix, especially when pumping, with mid-size aggregate such as ⅜" rock. Think of it as minimizing the size of void spaces that the cement/fly ash paste has to fill.

H. Pumping HFA Concrete

There are two particular benefits to pumping HFAC. One is that the longer set time allows wet concrete to remain longer in the hose lines without setting up while switching trucks. The other is the cohesion and workability, which makes the mix easier on pumps (and people!).

The best pump delivery system for HFAC is a 4″- to 6″-diameter hose from a boom truck. There should be no problem moving any mix design with a 3″ or higher slump through a 4″-diameter hose.

Concrete pumps with a 3″ hose will have some challenges, especially with hose lengths beyond 50 feet. At start-up, the development of rock pockets in the hose is not uncommon. Here are a few solutions:

- Reduce the ratio of rock (three fourths inch +) to gravel (three eighths inch). Many mix designs specify a high ratio of three fourths inch rock to gravel (e.g., 1500 lbs. rock to 400 lbs. gravel). Try changing that, for instance, to 1140 lbs. rock to 760 lbs. gravel.

- Run a bit of pure portland-cement slurry through the hose before the HFAC. This can often be accomplished by simply pouring a bag of portland cement into the hopper at the start of operations.

- If the concrete pump truck is coming from another job site, have them leave a load of mud in the hopper and use that to lubricate all the hose lines before pumping HFAC through them.

I. Health considerations

Fly ash should be treated and handled like cement. You don't want people handling it bare-handed, and you especially don't want them to breathe it.

A concern periodically arises that fly ash might be radioactive, and thus produce radioactive concrete. This is theoretically possible, in that some known coal deposits are interlaced with radioactive elements. The coal from such deposits, if mined and burned, would probably yield radioactive fly ash. That could happen in areas where such issues are not regulated, but in North America and the industrialized world in general, such coal is off-limits to mining simply because of the obvious health hazard to miners. To the best of this author's knowledge, none of the ashes on the market today are radioactive.

**BURNABY SKYTRAIN,
VANCOUVER, B.C., 2000**

50% fly ash replacement used in the poured-in-place footings, walls, columns, slabs, and stairways, and 30% fly ash replacement in precast elements

6

*It wasn't raining when
Noah built the ark.*

– Howard Ruff

WHY USE FLY ASH?

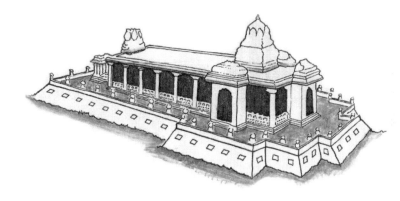

As we have seen, there are many practical reasons to add some (if not a lot of) fly ash to concrete–not just in addition to portland cement, but in *replacement* of it. In Chapter 3, we looked at the performance-enhancing effects of fly ash on workability, pumpability, strength, shrinkage, and permeability.

IRAIVAN TEMPLE, KAUAI, HAWAI'I, 2001

60% fly ash replacement used in the unreinforced 60' x 130' x 4' thick mat slab foundation, with no cracking and better-than-specified strength

The effects are so many, and so positive, that senior figures in the world of concrete have recently stated that concrete *without* fly ash belongs in a museum.

This may come as shocking news to many engineers, who remain convinced that fly ash in some way "waters down" the quality of concrete. When, as a junior engineer, I first heard of fly ash in the early 1980s, my supervisor sneeringly referred to it as "hamburger helper" or "filler." Those early impressions are sometimes hard to change, and they still linger in many parts of the concrete industry. In large part, those impressions are based on decades-old experience using ashes from earlier generations of power plants; those fly ashes were both coarser and higher in carbon residue than those commonly found today, and were thus much less effective as pozzolans. In another case, a 40% fly ash concrete was poured in 1981 for the Monterey Bay Aquarium using a superplasticizer. The project was ultimately successful, but incorrect dosages of the water-reducer caused premature gelling of the concrete; it started to set in the buckets before being emplaced, leaving in many people's minds the false impression that the high volume of fly ash was to blame. As anyone in construction knows, you can screw up anything if you're not paying attention, just as you can learn from mistakes (and are foolish if you don't) if you take the time to study what went wrong. What is generally true in construction is particularly so for concrete: you get what you *inspect*, not what you *expect*.

The big picture

Many reasons for using fly ash are global, environmental, or societal in nature. The production of portland cement puts about a ton of carbon dioxide (CO_2, a primary greenhouse gas) into the atmosphere for every ton of cement produced—roughly half a ton from the fuel used to cook the raw limestone, and half a ton from the calcination of the limestone. Worldwide, the production of portland cement alone accounts for 6-8% of human-generated CO_2 (depending on whom you ask). So here, in a single industry, lies the opportunity to slow the very alarming trend toward global warming. According to one authority:

> For every ton of fly ash used [to replace portland cement]—
> * Enough energy is saved to provide electricity to an average American home for 24 days.
> * The landfill space conserved equals 455 days of solid waste produced by the average American.
> * The reduction in CO_2 emissions equals 2 months of emissions from an automobile.

The cement industry deserves great credit for recognizing this, and for taking many effective steps to reduce its local and global environmental impacts. But the fact remains that we have a readily available industrial waste product—fly ash—that happens to be a perfect replacement for half or more of the cement in almost any mix, and yields equal or better-quality concrete. This is why high usage of fly ash in concrete is now a component for global trading of so-called "carbon credits," based on the Kyoto Accords and the Chicago Climate Exchange. Use of fly ash is also a means of making points in the increasingly important LEED™ (Leadership in Energy and Environmental Building) system of evaluating and rating buildings, developed by the US Green Building Council (USGBC). (For more detailed information, see the USGBC website at www.usgbc.org, and appendix C in this book for more elaboration and a sample calculation.)

Most of the fly ash produced today is currently being either landfilled, as in North America where lack of convenient rail spurs hinders bringing it to the marketplace, or simply flying freely out the smokestack of the coal-fired power plant from which it comes, as in China and India. Fly ash in the ground can pollute groundwater with heavy metals, while fly ash in the air constitutes particulate pollution—the bulk of the famous smog blanketing Beijing and many other cities that is a health hazard to everyone nearby. Fly ash trace metals and particulates cast into concrete, by contrast, are bound forever in a way that cannot hurt anyone.

Some in the green building movement question whether increasing the use of fly ash in concrete will effectively encourage coal-fired power production—itself a primary source of environmental degradation, pollution, and greenhouse gases. However, in light of the huge percentage of worldwide electricity generation *already* derived from coal, and the fact that so little of the ash currently being produced is stored safely in concrete, and the fact that both coal-fired power and concrete production are rapidly increasing along with the population, this seems like a weak argument at best. Current annual world production of cementitious and pozzolanic by-products of thermal power plants and metallurgical industries is about 650 million metric tons, of which only about 7% is being used by the cement and concrete industries. This is beyond wasteful; it is ridiculous. Simple arithmetic shows that coal and other fossil fuels have little or no place in the 100+ year plan for humanity. But for now and the next generation or two, we have the ash and we should use it intelligently. We can go on letting the existing output of fly ash be a landfill, pollution, and health problem, or we can use it to make better concrete.

There is also an enormous economic consideration in using fly ash. Portland cement-based concrete is the most ubiquitous construction material used in the United States and the world; currently more that 118 million tons are poured annually in the US, with fly ash now used to replace over 15 million tons of portland cement per year. Even so, in 2003 over 15 million tons of cement were imported into the US to make up for a shortage of native cement production. If domestic ash had replaced those imports, the result would have been an improvement in the US balance of trade of at least $1 billion. In a similar fashion, populous nations such as Brazil, India, and China are making or importing cement at great cost while grossly underutilizing their own native sources of ash and other industrial pozzolans. Things are, unfortunately, never quite so simple. For example, the cost of installing equipment to collect fly ash at the power plant is huge, and typically deemed uneconomical; what makes good business sense to the power plant owner is a disaster for society. Resolving a disparity like that—striking a balance between unfettered free-market capitalism and the need to protect the public welfare—can only be done in the societal and political arena.

Radically increasing the use of fly ash in concrete—whether blended at the ready-mix plant, or premixed and bagged at cement plants—is but one component of the broader effort to make concrete a more environmentally friendly building material without sacrificing quality or affordability. Other aspects in development include the use of other industrial by-products as cementitious materials or as components of cement manufacturing, the use of pervious concrete to absorb storm water, the use of light or white concrete to reduce the urban heat-island effect, and the reuse of demolished concrete as aggregate in new structures.

The widespread use of high fly ash concrete is an idea whose time has come. After decades of development in laboratories all over the world, and more recent use in demanding and varied projects, HFAC is now very much in the "real world" of concrete. In the preceding pages you saw how it works, how to use it, and pitfalls to avoid. In the references to follow you will find more technical detail.

Here is your start, and some tools to help. Good luck with your projects.

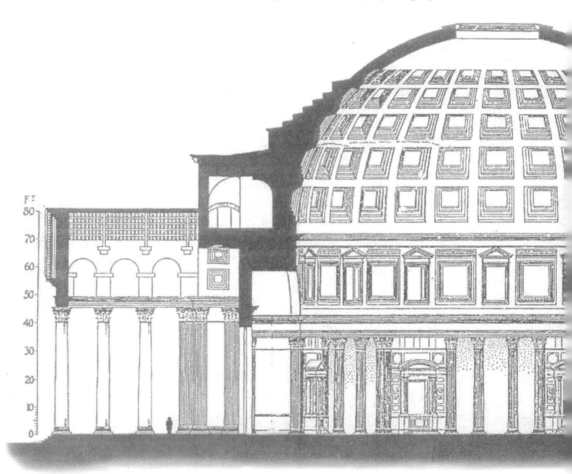

Sample Mix Designs

Notes from fly ash suppliers based on extensive field experience:

1. A 6-sack (cement + fly ash) mix design is a great place to start.

2. A 0.45 W/CM ratio will satisfy most job requirements, and, as one fly ash supplier noted, *"A W/CM well below 0.40 is a guaranteed way to make everybody's life miserable."* In other words, use a very low water content only if really necessary and if everyone understands the effects and is willing to do the extra work required.

3. A 4-6-oz/cubic yard dosage of a mid-range water reducer will suffice most of the time. Stay away from normal water reducers; if you can't, dose only to the cement (not total cementitious materials).

The following are some sample mix designs that have worked under particular conditions:

1

Portland cement	294 lbs
Fly ash (type not given)	306 lbs
Blended sand	1503 lbs
Crushed limestone	1750 lbs
Free water	199 lbs
High-range water reducer	14.4 oz/cwt
Air	1.2%
W/CM ratio	.33
Slump	9"
Unit weight	151 pcf
Initial set time (hours:minutes)	6 hr 20 min
Final set time (hours:minutes)	8 hr 00 min
COMPRESSIVE STRENGTH	PSI
1 day	1790
3 days	3660
7 days	4240
28 days	7770
56 days	8650
90 days	9290

Source: *Use of High Volume Fly Ash Concrete in the Real World* Copeland, Obla, and Meyer, San Antonio Texas

2

Type II portland cement	270 lbs
Class F Fly ash	329 lbs
Sand	1431 lbs
1" aggregate	1470 lbs
⅜" aggregate	450 lbs
Free water	200 lbs
High range water reducer	6-8 oz/cwt
Air	0%
W/CM ration	.33
Slump	5"
Unit weight (pcf)	
COMPRESSIVE STRENGTH	PSI
2 days	1350
3 days	1605
7 days	2110
14 days	2950
28 days	4660
56 days	5160
90 days	5670

Source: *Experience of a Quality Assurance Agency with High Volume Fly Ash Concrete in Northern California* Manmohan and Mehta, Berkeley, California

3

note: no water-reducing agents

Portland cement	300 lbs
Fly ash (type not given)	300 lbs
Blended sand	1230 lbs
⅜″ aggregate	575 lbs
1″ aggregate	1324 lbs
Free water	257 lbs
W/CM ratio	.43
Slump	6″
Initial set time (hours:minutes)	7 hr 35 min
COMPRESSIVE STRENGTH	PSI
3 days	1070
7 days	1550
14 days	1990
29 days	2730
56 days	4450

Source: *High Volume Fly Ash Concrete—*
Experience of a Ready-Mixed Concrete Producer
Burt Lockwood and Brian Adams, September 2001

4

note: using an accelerating agent

Type I/II portland cement	300 lbs
Class F Fly ash	300 lbs
Sand	1400 lbs
1″ aggregate	1500 lbs
⅜″ aggregate	400 lbs
Free water	280 lbs
Mid-range water reducer	5 oz/cwt
Accelerating mixture	10 oz/cwt
W/CM ration	.40
COMPRESSIVE STRENGTH	PSI
28 days	3000

Source: *HVFA in Custom Residential Projects*
Canyon Construction, October, 2004

5

note: this one used extremely careful curing in warm, moist climate (Kaui'i)

(see illustration on page 31)

portland cement	180 lbs
Class F Fly ash	240 lbs
Blended sand (lb./cubic yd., typ)	1600 lbs
1″ aggregate	1900 lbs
Free water	170 lbs
W/CM ration	.40
Normal water reducer	20 oz/yd
High range water reducer	90 oz/yd³
Slump	5-6″
COMPRESSIVE STRENGTH	PSI
3 days	968
7 days	1440
28 days	2343
90 days	3675

Source: *Microstructure of Concrete from a Crack-Free Structure*
Designed to Last a Thousand Years
John Asselanis and P. Kumar Mehta, September 2001

NOTES:

1. to convert from lbs./cubic yard to kgs./cubic meter, multiply by 0.5933
2. "oz/cwt" is ounces per hundred pounds (of cement)

Resources

Web

CANMET (Natural Resources Canada, a leading research organization):
www.nrcan.gc.ca/mms/canmet

Ecosmart (assistance with blended cements and pozzolanic concrete):
www.ecosmart.ca

American Concrete Institute: www.aci-int.org

American Coal Ash Association: www.acaa-usa.org

Electric Power Research Institute (EPRI): www.epri.com

Ecological Building Network: www.ecobuildnetwork.org

Environmental Building News: www.buildinggreen.com

Headwaters Resources (primary source of North American fly ash):
www.flyash.com/flyashconcrete.asp

TecEco Technologies (Australian research into alternative binders):
www.tececo.com

And you can search the Web for lots more.

Print

Malhotra, V.M. and Mehta, P.K., *Pozzolanic and Cementitious Materials*

Malhotra, V.M. and Mehta, P.K., *High Performance, High-Volume Fly Ash Concrete*

ACI Committee 232, *Fly Ash and Natural Pozzolans in Concrete*

American Concrete Institute, *Cementitious Materials for Concrete,* ACI Education
Bulletin No. E3-01. (…and many other publications; see www.aci-int.org)

Malin, Nadav, "The Fly Ash Revolution: Making Better Concrete with Less
Cement," *Environmental Building News,* V. 8, No. 6, June 1999.

CANMET/ACI International Conference Proceedings on *Fly Ash, Silica Fume,
Slag and Natural Pozzolans in Concrete* (First through Eighth, most recently May,
2004).

CANMET/ACI International Symposia on *Sustainable Development of Cement and
Concrete* (First through Third, most recently September, 2001).

Concrete, Fly Ash, and the Environment, Conference Proceedings, San Francisco, CA
(December 8, 1998).

Wilson, Alex, "Cement and Concrete: Environmental Considerations,"
Environmental Building News, V. 2, No. 2 (March/April, 1993).

High Fly Ash Concrete and LEED™

Courtesy of Horst, Inc.
A 7group Company
183 West Main Street
Kutztown, PA 19530
610-683-5730
www.sevengroup.com
www.coolclimateconcrete.com

The U.S. Green Building Council (USGBC) developed the LEED™ (Leadership in Energy & Environmental Design) Green Building Rating System to provide a national standard for green buildings. Today there are several LEED rating systems, including LEED for New Construction, LEED for Commercial Interiors, LEED for Existing Buildings and LEED for Core & Shell. LEED for Residential is due to premier at about the same time (late Spring of 2005) as this book is published, and there also are LEED certifications for design professionals. LEED standards are generally thought to be fairly complex and burdensome to the user—an oft-heard complaint, anyway—but they are expected to simplify as they evolve from these first attempts at quantifying what is and is not "green".

The LEED rating system for buildings allows users to earn points for satisfying credits. LEED for New Construction (LEED-NC) Version 2.1 has credits in five basic categories including Sustainable Sites, Water Efficiency, Energy & Atmosphere, Materials & Resources and Indoor Environmental Quality. An additional section provides credits for Innovation & Design Process. Applicants can attain different levels of USGBC certification dependent on the number of points the building has earned out of the 69 total possible points. The four levels of LEED-NC certification are:

LEED Certified (26 to 32 points)

LEED Silver (33 to 38 points)

LEED Gold (39 to 51 points)

LEED Platinum (52 points and higher)

Concrete and concrete products can contribute both directly and indirectly towards earning points in several LEED credits. In some cases, concrete products help earn the point because of their properties; in others, the use of concrete products means

that other materials do not have to be used. It is important to understand that single products do not achieve LEED credits. Single products, such as concrete, however, can be used strategically and in conjunction with other materials and technologies to achieve a variety of credits.

Specific LEED-NC credits – Direct concrete contribution

Sustainable Sites Credit 7.1: Landscape & Exterior Design to Reduce Heat Islands

The intent of this credit is to reduce heat islands—locally warmed air—to minimize the impact on microclimate and human and wildlife habitat. There are several alternative requirements to meet this credit, one of which is providing shade and/or using high-albedo material with a reflectance of at least 0.3 for at least 30% of the site's non-roof impervious surfaces. This credit is often achieved through the use of concrete with a reflectance of at least 0.3. As described in the text, fly ash tends to lighten the color of concrete, ie raise its albedo.

To calculate whether this credit has been achieved, a project team first calculates the total square footage of non-roof impervious surfaces on the LEED site. This typically includes parking lots, walkways and other paved areas. If concrete has been used for at least 30% of this square footage, the credit has been earned.

Materials & Resources Credit 4: Recycled Content

The intent of this credit is to increase demand for building products that incorporate recycled content materials, therefore reducing impacts resulting from extraction and processing of virgin materials. This credit is incremental with a possibility of earning two points. The first point is earned if the value of post-consumer recycled content plus one-half of the value of post-industrial content of project materials constitutes at least 5% of the total value of the materials in the project. A second point is earned if the 10% level is reached. (Stated simply, "post-industrial" is what's left over at the factory after the product or material is shipped out; "post-consumer" is what's left over after the consumer has used the product or material.)

Concrete that contains fly ash or ground granulated blast furnace slag (GGBFS) can help contribute towards achievement of this credit, since both fly ash and GGBFS are post-industrial recycled materials. To calculate this credit, project teams determine the total cost of materials for the project (excluding labor). Alternatively, proj-

ect teams can base the calculations for this credit on a default materials cost, which is determined based on the total project cost. Once the total material cost is established, project teams determine which materials contain post-consumer and/or post-industrial recycled content and how much by weight each contains. Dollar values are then assigned to the recycled content, and the total recycled content value of all materials is added together and compared to the total materials cost. These calculations are often done in a materials spreadsheet or on the LEED Letter Template that has built in calculations. The LEED Letter Template also provides a default total materials cost if the total materials cost is not available.

For example, if concrete with fly ash is used on a project, the first step would be to determine how much recycled content the concrete contains. Assuming that fly ash makes up approximately 6% by weight of the concrete mix, and fly ash is a 100% post-industrial recycled material, the concrete has a 6% post-industrial recycled content. If the material cost for concrete is $500,000, then the dollar value of the recycled content is $500,000* .06 divided by 2, which is $15,000. Remember, since the recycled content is post-industrial, the value is divided in half, because the credit threshold is based on the value of post-consumer + *one-half* of the value of post-industrial. Let's say that the project team determined that the recycled content value of all materials combined was $150,000, and the total materials cost for the project is $2,000,000. The project will achieved a recycled content percentage of 7.5% and one point will be awarded.

Materials & Resources Credit 5: Local/Regional Materials

The intent of this credit is to increase demand for building materials and products that are extracted and manufactured with the region, thereby supporting the regional economy and reducing the environmental impacts resulting from transportation. This credit has two components. To earn the first point, a minimum of 20% of building materials and products must be manufactured regionally within a radius of 500 miles. To earn the second point, a minimum of 10% of building materials and products must be extracted, harvested, or recovered within 500 miles of the project site in addition to being locally manufactured.

Since use of concrete is regional, concrete products often contribute toward earning both points of this credit. To do so, concrete manufacture must take place within 500 miles of the project site and all raw materials used in the concrete must be harvested or extracted within a 500 mile radius of the project site.

To calculate this credit, project teams determine the total cost of materials for the project (excluding labor). Alternatively, as with the recycled content credit, project teams can base the calculations for this credit on a default materials cost, which is determined based on the total project cost. Once the total material cost is established, project teams determine which materials are locally manufactured and which are both locally manufactured AND locally harvested or extracted. The total value of locally manufactured materials is compared to the total materials cost. If the locally manufactured materials constitute 20% or more of the total materials cost, the first point is earned. Likewise, if the locally harvested or extracted materials constitute 10% of the total materials cost, the second point is earned.

As an example, suppose the materials cost for cast-in-place concrete for a project in Newark, NJ is $325,000. The concrete was manufactured at a nearby ready-mix plant, and all of the raw materials, including aggregates and cements, came from within 200 miles of Newark, NJ. The project team has calculated that in addition to the concrete, $425,000 worth of other materials are locally manufactured, and $175,000 worth are both locally manufactured and harvested. Based on a total materials cost of $2,500,000, $750,000 or 30% of materials are locally manufactured, earning the first point. $500,000, or 20% are both locally manufactured and harvested, earning the second point.

Innovation & Design Process Credit 1: Innovation in Design

The intent of this credit is to provide design teams and projects with the opportunity to be awarded points for exceptional performance above the requirements set by the LEED Green Building Rating System and/or innovative performance in Green Building categories not specifically addressed by the LEED Green Building Rating System. There is an established innovation credit based on reducing the amount of Portland cement used in a project's concrete mixes. To earn this credit, a 40% reduction in Portland cement use in cast-in-place concrete must be documented beyond a baseline amount. In order to obtain this innovation credit point, a minimum of 40% reduction of CO_2 by weight for all cast-in-place concrete must be demonstrated against standard baseline mixes. Cast-in-place concrete must make up a significant portion of the work on the project.

For purposes of this credit, the following must be applied:
- One pound of Portland cement is equivalent to one pound of CO_2.
- Baseline mixes shall be standard, 28-day strength regional mix designs.

- Temperature range shall be accounted for and documented. Documentation for cold weather mix designs shall include temperature on day of pour.
- Pozzolans and other cementitious materials allowed for displacement of Portland cement include fly ash, ground granulated blast furnace slag, silica fume and rice hull ash.

Steps to achieving the blended cement innovation point:

1. Review the Credit Interpretation Ruling (CIR) dated 01/23/03, available on the USGBC website www.usgbc.org
2. Determine what pozzolans or other cementitious materials are available based on the project location.
3. Obtain technical advice to determine feasibility. Pozzolan suppliers and ACI literature (and other references listed in Appendix B) can provide test data for wary structural engineers and ready mix suppliers. These sources can also help determine if 40% or more replacement is technically sound given project specifics.
4. Discuss the credit in an initial charrette or LEED goal setting session.
5. Research which concrete companies in the project area are capable of providing storage for specified materials.
6. Determine baseline mixes based on regional requirements and date of pour.
7. Establish which portions of the mix should contain specific amounts of portland cement (e.g. footings, ground slabs, elevated slabs, columns, insulating concrete forms or blocks)
8. Write specifications to reflect calculated amounts which achieve 40% or more total replacement compared to the baseline.
9. Provide narrative and calculations as documentation.

The following calculation reflects a ninety thousand square foot project being poured in winter in an area that has high freeze/thaw conditions.

A	B	C	D	E	F	G	E	F
Design Mix	Strength psi	Quantity poured for project (cy)	fly ash in project mix design (lbs/cy)	fly ash in project mix design (lbs)	portland cement in project mix design (lbs/cy)	portland cement in project mix design (lbs)	Baseline portland cement mix (lbs/cy)	Baseline portland cement (lbs)
#1	4,000	696	300	208,701	300	208,701	600	417,402
#2	4,000	369	210	77,454	390	143,844	600	221,298
#3	4,000	2,708	150	406,250	450	1,218,749	650	1,760,415
#4	4,000	21	60	1,278	540	11,502	650	13,845
#5	3,000	41	260	10,660	260	10,660	500	20,500
#6	4,000	1,187	360	427,237	240	284,825	600	712,062
TOTAL		5,022		1,131,580		1,878,280		3,145,522

Reduction in portland cement (lbs)   1,267,241.50
Percentage reduction in portland cement   40.49%

Specific LEED-NC credits – Indirect concrete contribution

The following examples illustrate how concrete can indirectly contribute towards the achievement of credits or points. In the Sustainable Sites section of LEED, concrete is often used in various aspects of stormwater management. Obviously concrete in itself does not constitute stormwater management but a sound stormwater management plan may very well include the use of concrete.

Another example is the Optimize Energy Performance credit in the Energy & Atmosphere section. The intent of this credit is to achieve increasing levels of energy performance above the prerequisite standard to reduce environmental impacts associated with excessive energy use. This is an important credit in LEED as up to ten points can be earned in the credit. There are many ways to achieve increased levels of energy performance, including examining building orientation for proper solar exposure and careful planning of the building envelope. An integrated strategy to address energy performance could include (but does not require), among other strategies, the use of Insulated Concrete Forms (ICFs) in combination with good roof insulation, energy efficient fenestration, lighting design that lowers the amount of light and heat generated in the building, daylighting that works in combination with the lighting design, efficient equipment and a variety of other factors. When all of these factors are integrated, increased energy performance can often be achieved.

Another example of the use of concrete to indirectly contribute toward credit achievement is in Indoor Environmental Quality Credit 4: Low-Emitting Materials. The intent of this credit is to reduce the quantity of indoor air contaminants that are odorous, potentially irritating and/or harmful to the comfort and well-being of installers and occupants. The four points within this credit are earned for using adhesives, sealants, paints, coatings, carpet and composite wood that meet various standards. Concrete can often indirectly function as a way to achieve these points since with the use of a proper sealer, concrete can serve as a finish material and thus eliminate the need for other materials that would have indoor contaminants associated with them. For example, a concrete finished floor with a water based sealer would mean that other flooring products would not need to be used. So in this example concrete is not achieving the credit but it allows for the non-use of other materials that would require strict adherence to air quality standards.

Other LEED ratings systems

The other LEED rating systems, including LEED for Commercial Interiors, LEED for Existing Buildings and LEED for Core & Shell, are similar in structure to LEED for New Construction in that they allow users to earn points for satisfying credits. Credits are also similarly grouped in categories, but specific credits vary by rating system, as do the number of points available and certification thresholds. Many of the credits outlined above are found in one or several of these rating systems. The rating system where concrete and concrete products are likely to be the most relevant is LEED for Core & Shell, currently in its pilot phase, which addresses sustainable design in new core and shell construction. As defined by the USGBC, "core and shell construction covers base building elements, such as the structure, envelope and building-level systems, such as central HVAC, etc" which means that concrete is likely a significant material in these building projects.

The Art & Science of
Building Well

ABOUT GREEN BUILDING PRESS

The term "green building" has recently entered the popular lexicon, though not in any well-defined way. Like beauty, its significance is in the eye of the beholder. For some, the term requires articulating in detail the philosophy and goals of "sustainable" or "regenerative" design, and there is already a vigorous and healthy public discourse on what those terms might connote. For others, green building means healthy, non-toxic building interiors that don't poison their occupants, or a vigorous switch away from fossil-fuel dependence to energy-efficiency and renewable energy sources, or even the radical notion that the shape, materials, and electromagnetic fields of buildings have effects, rarely quantifiable, on the physical, emotional and spiritual well-being of occupants—effects that deserve more than a little scrutiny. There are also those who measure the effects of buildings on their immediate environs as a benchmark of greenness—heat island effects in cities (where most humans now live), urban runoff effects on waterways, and the effects of the construction industry, in its immense scale and variety, on the planet-wide ecosystem that is unmetaphorically our life support system.

All of the above deserves serious attention, but it is not material for Green Building Press—though, to one degree or another, all such discussions form the intellectual corpus that underlies and overarches our work. There is theory and there is practice; we are about practice. We are where the rubber meets the road. We seek to specifically identify where our regular ways of building are, in fact, harmful or just don't work, and then specifically describe viable improvements. Others have written passionately, extensively, and articulately on the need to save at least a few patches of wild forest from the axe; we write of alternatives—there are many!—to using wood in buildings. Others may write the obscure but necessary academic papers on, say, variations in chloride-ion permeability of early-age concrete mixes containing varying amounts of fly ash; we write about improving concrete for the builder who has to pour 1600 cubic yards of foundation in the next three weeks or face ruinous financial penalties. That builder may not even know what chloride-ion permeability is; what matters is getting a lot of mud into the forms without breaking the pumps, losing strength, or creating excessive void pockets. It is, to the best of our ability, to that person that we address our work, as well as to the engineers and architects straightjacketed by the "standard of care" and overwhelmingly compelled by legal, cultural, and psychological forces to keep doing what everyone else is doing.

We—the builders, architects, and engineers who write for Green Building Press—see ways to improve the way we build, and we seek to bring those to your attention in the simplest and easiest-to-use ways we can. Just as we cannot live without causing harm, from the worms and insects we step on to the cows and cabbages we eat, we cannot build without causing harm. But we can look for ways to cause the *least* harm in our work, and even to build in a manner that regenerates life and landscapes; this is what we mean by "improve." We see this simply as good business. If nothing else, we seek to respect our descendants and the world they will inherit. Recognize and learn from our mistakes, then correct and move forward; that is the art and science of building well.

Visit us at **www.greenbuildingpress.com**

About Bruce King

After graduating from the University of Colorado in Architectural Engineering, Bruce King worked on houses, hospitals, high-rise structures, airplanes and Polynesian resorts before obtaining his license in 1983 and starting his own engineering consultancy. Since 1989 that business has been based in Sausalito, California, from which he also directs the non-profit Ecological Building Network (www.ecobuildnetwork.org) which he founded in 1999. He is also the author of *Buildings of Earth and Straw/Structural Design for Rammed Earth and Straw Bale Architecture,* and along with his wife, Sarah, is the founder and owner of Green Building Press. He is very fortunate to live with, support, and be supported by his wife, son, daughter, and poodle in a lovely little valley draining to the San Francisco Bay.

The monk asked,
"How is it when the trees wither, and the leaves fall?"
Yunmen replied,
"Body exposed to the Golden Wind."

— from the *Blue Cliff Record*